PEACE PEN PALS

HOPING FOR PEACE IN
SUDAN

Divided by conflict, wishing for peace

by Jim Pipe

Gareth Stevens
Publishing

Please visit our website, www.garethstevens.com. For a free color catalog of all our high-quality books, call toll free 1-800-542-2595 or fax 1-877-542-2596.

Library of Congress Cataloging-in-Publication Data

Pipe, Jim, 1966-
Hoping for peace in Sudan / Jim Pipe.
    p. cm. — (Peace pen pals)
Includes index.
ISBN 978-1-4339-7740-4 (pbk.)
ISBN 978-1-4339-7741-1 (6-pack)
ISBN 978-1-4339-7739-8 (library binding)
1. Sudan—History—Civil War, 1983-2005—Peace—Juvenile literature. 2. Sudan—History—Darfur Conflict, 2003—Peace—Juvenile literature. I. Title. II. Series: Peace pen pals.
DT157.672.P57 2012
962.404—dc23

2012003488

First Edition

Published in 2013 by
Gareth Stevens Publishing
111 East 14th Street, Suite 349
New York, NY 10003

© 2013 Gareth Stevens Publishing

Produced by Calcium, www.calciumcreative.co.uk
Designed by Paul Myerscough
Edited by Sarah Eason and Laura Waxman
Picture research by Susannah Jayes

Photo credits: Cover: Dreamstime: John Wollwerth br; Shutterstock: Ryan Rodrick Beiler/Shinelu bg, Urosr bl. Inside: Bertramz: 36br; Corinthia Hotels: 14b; Maureen Didde 17c; Petr Adam Dohnálek: 8t, 34br, 35tr; Dreamstime: Kobby Dagan 19tr, Dicogm 39tr, Dreamshot 41cl, 46tr, Ferdinandreus 16b, Matt Fowler 11tr, 19br, 22t, 27b, 29t, 37c, Johnnymitch 3b, 21tr, Rosaria Meneghello 30b, Savagelioness 9tl, David Snyder 18b, 23cr, 31tr, John Wollwerth 7c, 38cl, 41br, 42t; Istockphoto: Claudia Dewald 4b, 6b, Mina Fouad 15b, Jean Nordmann 13tr, GYI NSEA 24br, 25tr, Phototreat 9b, Uros Ravbar 5t; Shutterstock: Africa924 32t, 44b, Ilya Andriyanov 3, Frontpage 10br, 12b, 43c, Sergey Lavrentev 10–11c, Oleg_Mit 39cl, Zoltan Pataki 39tl, Urosr 33tr, Tomasz Wieja 10 background; USAID: 26bc, 28b.

Printed in the United States of America

CPSIA compliance information: Batch #CS12GS: For further information contact Gareth Stevens, New York, New York at 1-800-542-2595.

CONTENTS

WAR-TORN SUDAN

For nearly 30 years, stories from Sudan have made the headlines. The world watched as a terrible civil war tore the country apart. Today, the worst of the fighting is over, but although there is peace, it is uncertain. In 2011, South Sudan voted to split from the northern part of the country.

People have been living in the region since the time of the ancient Egyptians in around 2000 BC. Around 1,200 years ago, the Arabs invaded northern Sudan, bringing Islam with them. In the 1500s, other peoples, such as the Dinka and Nuer, settled further south.

Most people in South Sudan live in small towns and villages, many without basic services such as safe drinking water and electricity.

Sudan has an ancient past. The pyramids of Meroë were built around 2,000 years ago as tombs for kings and queens.

Fighting Breaks Out

The British colonized part of Sudan in the late 1800s, but in 1956, modern Sudan declared its independence. Soon after, a civil war started between the people living in the south and those in the north. After a peace deal, the south ruled itself for most of the 1970s. Fighting broke out again in 1983. The conflict then lasted for more than 20 years.

AN ENORMOUS COUNTRY

Sudan is Africa's largest country. The far north is largely dry, hot desert, with giant dust storms called haboobs. The center of the country is mostly grassland. The south is tropical with forests and a huge swamp known as the Sudd. The Nile River, the longest river in the world, runs through the whole country. These varied landscapes are home to many different peoples, each with their own languages and traditions.

CHAPTER ONE

NORTH VS SOUTH

During the 1980s and 1990s, Sudan's civil war ravaged an already poor country. More than 2 million Sudanese people died in the conflict, and around 4 million others were forced from their homes.

The south is mostly populated by black Africans who live in the countryside and follow Christian or traditional African religions. Arabs live in the north, with many in cities such as the capital, Khartoum, and Port Sudan. Many of the Arab Sudanese are Muslims.

Since independence, the southerners have struggled against control by the north. In 1983, a southerner named John Garang organized a rebel army called the Sudanese People's Liberation Army (SPLA). Its troops launched attacks on government forces in the north.

During the civil war, there was bitter fighting between government forces and rebel troops. However, many more people died from famine and disease.

When the government fought back against the rebels, the country was plunged into a civil war.

Drought and Famine

To add to the misery, a lack of rain led to a drought in Sudan during the mid-1980s, the worst in the country's history. More than 4.5 million people were badly affected.

The United Nations and other international organizations tried to help by sending food supplies and emergency medicine. However, government troops stopped the supplies from reaching rebel areas in the south. Thousands died from famine or disease. Poor harvests led to further famines in 1991 and then in 1998, ravaging the country again.

Many villagers in South Sudan make a living by herding cattle. Bad droughts can lead to violence as neighboring groups try to steal each other's cattle.

FLOODS

In 1988, heavy rains caused massive flooding in the north. More than 2 million people fled from Khartoum, and over 120,000 homes were destroyed, leaving 750,000 Sudanese people homeless. Millions more were left without food.

This bustling marketplace is a typical sight in the Arab towns and cities of northern Sudan.

The People of Sudan

The local nickname for Sudan, "laham ras," describes a popular meat dish filled with many different flavors and textures. Similarly, the country is home to 19 different peoples and 100 languages.

Black Africans

More than half of all Sudanese are black Africans. The largest groups are the Dinka and the Nuer, who live in the south. Traditionally, these peoples both herded cattle and competed for water supplies or places to graze their herds. During the civil war, the Dinka and Nuer sometimes fought each other as well as the government forces.

Also in the south are the Shilluk people, known for their farming and fishing skills. Another farming people, the Fur, are black African Muslims. They live in a western region known as Darfur. The Nubians are another Muslim community of black Africans mostly living in northern Sudan.

Arab Peoples

Although most people in northern and central Sudan are Arabs and Muslims, they come from a variety of ethnic groups and follow different ways of life. There are also nomads in Sudan, known as the Beja. In the last 20 years, many Beja have settled near Port Sudan.

SUDAN AND THE SUDANESE

Area of Sudan: 967,500 square miles
Population: 45 million
Capital city: Khartoum
Official language: Arabic
Religion: 70 percent of Sudanese people follow Islam, 25 percent follow traditional African religions. The rest are Christians.

Many children in Sudan start work at a very young age. These children are selling corn in Terekeka in South Sudan.

LIFE IN THE SOUTH

Mangalatore Refugee Camp,
Southern Sudan
March 1999
Dear Sittina,
    I am so glad for your letter. With all the fighting, I didn't expect it to arrive. Let me tell you about my people, the Dinka. We have been living near the Nile River for thousands of years. We call ourselves the Moinjaang, or "people of the people." We're very proud of our traditions, such as our poems, songs, and dances. Our life is simple. We herd cattle, grow crops, and fish.

Here is a picture of my village before the war. Every hut was home to a different family.

Cattle farming

Traditionally, cattle are very important to the Dinka people. They provide meat, milk, and butter, as well as leather for mats and drums. Horns and bones are carved into tools and musical instruments.

In the rainy season, we grow crops such as millet and sorghum.

For a long time, the Dinka were allowed to live in peace. Then civil war came, and everything changed. Arab raiders attacked villages in my area. My family was lucky to get away alive, but it was hard leaving our home behind. Some families fled to neighboring Kenya or Uganda. Others headed to Khartoum. As you know, my family fled to Ethiopia then ended up back here in Mangalatore, where I was born.

It sounds like many people in Khartoum are also hoping for an end to the war. I hope that one day there will be peace.

Write to me soon and tell me more about life in Khartoum. Can you send me a postcard so I can see what it looks like?

Your friend,

Manute

Islamic Law

Religious differences have played a big part in Sudan's troubles. The Muslim government in Khartoum tried to force Islamic laws on the whole country, contributing to the civil war between north and south.

Islam is Sudan's main religion, and over two-thirds of Sudanese people are Muslims. For them, Islamic prayer and rituals are an essential part of daily life.

In the south, millions of Sudanese follow traditional African beliefs. A smaller number are Christian. Many of those who follow Islam and Christianity also follow some of their ancient African beliefs.

In 1980s, however, the Sudanese government was run by Muslims with extreme religious views. In 1983, President Jaffar Nimeiri declared that citizens who did not follow Islamic law would

These Sudanese men are praying in the courtyard of a mosque. Muslim men and women pray in separate groups.

be punished. Many of these punishments were so incredibly harsh that Christians in the south decided to rebel against them.

In 1989, a new leader came to power in Sudan, Omar Hassan al-Bashir. He was supported by very strict Muslims. Al-Bashir fired thousands of people in the army, police force, and government and gave their jobs to Muslims. This enraged non-Muslims all over Sudan and caused even more tension.

South Sudanese Christians began to take up arms against the northern regime in protest against the harsh punishments imposed upon them.

RELIGIOUS PERSECUTION

Non-Muslims in Sudan have suffered in many ways. Many Muslim employers do not allow Christian employees time off to go to church on Sundays. Christian students are blocked from going to university, and the police hassle or arrest them if they wear western clothing, such as blue jeans.

LETTER FROM SITTINA

Khartoum
June 1999
Dear Manute,

I was very sad to hear about all the terrible things that are still going on in the south of Sudan. My father is very angry about the war. Although he is proud to be a Muslim, he believes everyone should be allowed to practice their own religion in peace. As you know, Khartoum is the second largest Muslim city in Africa, but since the war began many Christians from the south have also come to live here. My mother says there are more churches than ever.

The plush Cornitha hotel in Khartoum seems like it's on a different planet than war-torn southern Sudan.

Mosques

Mosques, Islamic places of worship, have been built in Sudan since the early days of Islam. There are many large and well-known mosques in Khartoum, some hundreds of years old. As well as being a place for prayer, many of the largest mosques are used as colleges or universities.

This is just one of the many mosques in Khartoum.

I can't believe we are living in the same country. Here in Khartoum, life is peaceful—apart from horns blaring in traffic jams. Sometimes we see soldiers on the streets, but so far there has been no fighting. It feels very safe.

Some days we visit the markets in Omdurman across the river. There is nothing you can't buy—even camels! Last week there were huge crowds in line to see a soccer match between two local teams.

Watching sports probably seems crazy to you while there is so much fighting in the south. Every night I think of you and hope that the war will be over soon.

Sittina

CHAPTER TWO

THE CHAOS OF WAR

The problems in Sudan are very complex. Although the war began as a clash between non-Muslims in the south and Muslims in the north, it spread into other parts of Sudan as old rivals took up arms against each other.

In 1991, when President Al-Bashir reinforced Islamic law in Sudan, the rebel forces split. Some rebels wanted to stay united with the north. Others thought southern Sudan should become independent. This disagreement led to even more bloodshed as the rebel groups began to fight each other.

Millions of Sudanese fled their homes during the civil war. Some traveled by truck, while others made long journeys on foot, on camels, or on carts.

The Rebellion Grows

In the early 1990s, Sudan's neighbors, including Ethiopia, Uganda, and Kenya, encouraged Sudan's government to end the war. In 1997, the government signed a cease-fire with some rebel groups, but the fighting continued. More and more groups in Sudan began to join the rebels, including the Muslim Nubians in the mountain regions of central Sudan.

In 2002, however, the Sudanese government met rebel leader John Garang for peace talks in Kenya. After much discussion, both sides agreed to end the war. By 2003, there were real hopes for peace in the war-torn country.

The Nuba mountains of central Sudan saw some of the fiercest fighting of the civil war, and for many years the region was cut off from the outside world.

LINKS TO TERRORISM

Many countries in the West stopped helping Sudan in the 1990s because of its links to terrorist groups. Osama bin Laden, who organized the 9/11 terrorist attacks on New York City, lived in Khartoum for several years in the 1990s. In 1998, the United States launched a missile attack on a factory in Khartoum that was linked to bin Laden.

Darfur

Just as Sudan's civil war seemed to be ending, fighting broke out in Darfur, a region in west Sudan about the size of Texas. For years, the local black Muslims had been having issues with Arab Muslim farmers over land and water. Finally, they decided to fight back.

In 2003, the black Muslim rebels attacked government troops and police stations in Darfur. They demanded more rights and a share of the money from the region's many valuable oil fields.

The government's response was swift and brutal. It supplied local Arab nomads with horses, camels, and weapons. Although these raiders, known as "janjaweed" (Arabic for "horse and gun"), soon defeated the rebels, they kept on raiding. Supported by the Sudanese army and air force, they destroyed village after village, burning, looting, and killing many people.

The conflict in Darfur has affected over 5 million people and created one of the world's worst refugee crises.

Victims of War

In Darfur, more than 300,000 people died as a result of the attacks, many from hunger and disease. Yet many Arab villages were untouched. This led the United Nations to believe that the janjaweed were deliberately trying to kill all the non-Arabs in Darfur.

The janjaweed also forced over 2.7 million people from their homes. Many of these refugees ended up in nearby camps. Even with aid from overseas, it was impossible to feed them all. The conflict in Darfur had become an even bigger problem than the original war itself.

Protesters in America demanded more action from the US government and the United Nations to stop the violence.

FLEEING TO CHAD

More than 200,000 people from Darfur fled across the border to Sudan's neighbor, Chad. They were chased by janjaweed raiders who also fought with Chadian government forces, almost starting another war.

ON THE RUN

Kakuma Refugee Camp in Kenya
June 2003
Dear Sittina,
I'm sorry it has taken so long to reply to your last letter. When I last wrote we were living in Mangalatore, but gradually things got too dangerous, and we decided to move to another camp.
Bad mistake. One night, the government forces attacked because they thought the camp was a rebel base. We heard lots of shouting and screaming. Soon the whole camp was on fire.

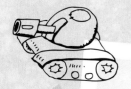

Rebel soldiers said they were fighting for freedom, but they also carried out terrible crimes.

The Lost Boys

More than 40,000 boys from southern Sudan, aged 4 to 15, lost their parents in the war. They survived by walking hundreds of miles to Ethiopia, then back to Sudan. Many ended up in the Kakuma Refugee Camp. Separated from their parents, families, and homes, they became known as the "Lost Boys" of Sudan.

Many orphaned children have forgotten their names and where they came from.

My family managed to escape, and we walked for many days in very hot weather. It was hard to find food or water, and we were very hungry and thirsty. In the end, my mother decided it was safest to cross the border. A boy we met told us about a camp called Kakuma in Kenya.

It is very hot and dry in Kakuma, with few trees and little grass, just tents and huts as far as the eye can see. Though it seems to be safe here, I find it very hard to go to sleep. I keep thinking about the night of the attack.

Now I understand why my uncles joined the rebel forces. But I do not think either side will ever win. Wars don't solve problems—they just create more.

Manute

21

Peacekeeping troops from the United Nations failed to stop the fighting between rebels and government forces in Darfur.

A Peace Deal

Despite the growing conflict in Darfur, the peace talks between the government in the north and the southern rebels continued. In early 2005, a new deal was reached after three years of negotiation. Finally, one of the longest civil wars in the world was over.

In July 2005, a crowd gathered in the center of Khartoum to celebrate a meeting between rebel leader John Garang and President Al-Bashir. The old rivals had agreed to share power and end Islamic law in the south. The south would also get half of Sudan's oil wealth. Three weeks later, Garang died in a helicopter crash during terrible weather, but the two sides decided to carry on the peace process he had begun.

Peace in Darfur

In Darfur, the janjaweed continued their brutal attacks on villages. After several delays, a joint force of 26,000 troops from the African Union and the United Nations was sent to Sudan to prevent further attacks and keep the peace.

However, in 2008, a rebel force from Darfur attacked Omdurman, just across the river from Khartoum. Though the attack failed, it was the first time fighting had come so close to the capital. This was a turning point. Alarmed by the proximity of the fighting, in 2010, President Al-Bashir signed the cease-fire with the Darfur rebels.

The violence in Darfur makes it difficult for aid agencies to provide refugees with a regular supply of food, water, and medicines.

DANGER IN DARFUR

By the end of the war in Darfur, millions of people were left homeless and underfed. Disease was another major problem. Overseas aid agencies were working in the region, but many people still suffered.

WHEN WILL IT END?

Khartoum
March 2004
Dear Manute,

I felt very sad reading your last letter. This war has been going on so long, and it's heartbreaking to think that things are actually getting worse for you.

I got into an argument at school recently when the subject of war came up. Many of the other girls don't really think about the war. When I asked them why it started, nobody seemed to know—or care. Maybe it's because Khartoum is such a long way from the fighting.

This busy car showroom shows how little people in Khartoum are affected by the war.

Building Up Khartoum

Although Khartoum is home to more than 5 million people, most buildings in the city were only one or two stories high. Since the peace deal was signed in 2005, several big building projects have taken place, including a new airport, a new bridge, and two luxurious hotels.

Khartoum is rapidly expanding.

When I asked the girls why there were huge refugee camps all around the city, they got very quiet. Every day, refugees from the south trek into Khartoum looking for work, but no one pays much attention to their suffering. Perhaps I should show my classmates your letters. Maybe then they would understand what has been going on.

I don't want to get your hopes up, but there have been several reports on the radio about peace talks between the rebels and the government. But I have also heard that a new war has started in the west, in Darfur, this time against other Muslims. Is our country never going to be at peace?

Sittina

CHAPTER THREE

DAILY STRUGGLES

The war brought countless problems for ordinary Sudanese people. Many villagers were often caught between the government forces and rebel fighters. Forces on all sides burned villages, destroyed crops, and stole cattle. The fighting also prevented food supplies and medicine from reaching refugees. All of this led to starvation and disease.

Even in peaceful times, the frequent droughts made life hard. With their homes destroyed or abandoned, it was almost impossible for villagers to grow crops, raise cattle, or earn money.

In some camps there are no materials to build even simple shelters.

Refugee Camps

Life in the refugee camps is particularly tough. People build their shacks with whatever they can find. Entire families live in tiny, dirty spaces. They have little food, no work, and virtually no privacy.

A typical day in the camp starts very early, usually with a long trek to get water. In the dry season, midday temperatures often reach 110°F. In the rainy season, food supplies are often delayed and the refugees go hungry. Sometimes rivers flood the camps.

KIDNAPPED CHILDREN

There have been many reports of Arab fighters kidnapping black African women and children from the south. Their victims are sold into slavery in the north to become servants, farm workers, or soldiers. Young boys have been trained to fight against their own people. After years of slavery, some children forget their real names and where they come from.

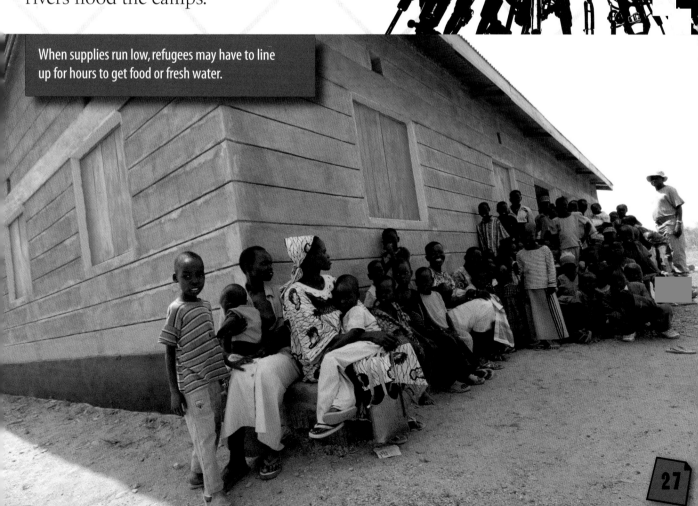

When supplies run low, refugees may have to line up for hours to get food or fresh water.

27

Caught Up in the Conflict

Most aspects of Sudanese life have been affected by the war. Thousands of homes need to be rebuilt, and crowded conditions in refugee camps have led to the spread of disease. A generation of Sudan's children, meanwhile, have grown up with little education.

Sudan has a very young population. Nearly half of the country's people are under the age of 15, and that number is likely to grow over the coming years.

The Sudanese believe that education is very important. A new school curriculum was developed for southern Sudan after the signing of the peace agreement. Yet a lack of money means many villages have no teachers or even classrooms. In the refugee camps, teachers do their best to teach the children with very few resources. Getting an education is tough.

Sudanese girls are expected to learn skills from their mothers or female relatives. However, the civil war has separated many young girls from families.

Even after the civil war ended, it was very hard to see a doctor in South Sudan. In 2012, there were just nine hospitals in the country.

Health Care

The health system in Sudan is poor, with few hospitals and health clinics in the countryside. There is also not enough medicine to deal with deadly diseases such as yellow fever and malaria. It is hard to obtain even simple medicine such as aspirin and other painkillers that can relieve suffering.

Waterborne diseases are another major problem, especially in southern Sudan. Only one in two people in the whole country has access to safe drinking water.

HIGH UNEMPLOYMENT

Jobs are scarce in Sudan, particularly for refugees. Many refugees have little or no education. Those that do have an education often have low-paying jobs on farms, in factories, or in schools in the camp.

LIFE IN A REFUGEE CAMP

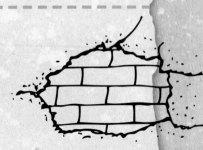

Kakuma Refugee Camp, Kenya
June 2006
Dear Sittina,
    We are still in the camp here in Kenya,
but now that peace has come to much of
Sudan, many people hope to return to their
homes. We are all still waiting for any news
about our families and villages.

Children are taught
in temporary outdoor
schools in refugee camps.

Simple Shelters

Some shelters in the refugee camps are built from sheets of iron while others are more like tents. The United Nations hands out poles and other materials so that people make more comfortable homes.

A bag of peanuts is a rare treat!

This place is windy, dry, and very hot. Although we are given food every day, I miss eating fresh fruit and vegetables. Some families have planted tiny vegetable plots, but you cannot grow much in the dry soil. With no cattle to herd, and no land to dig, many people have nothing to do all day.

There are many young boys here who have lost their parents. One of them, Dol, now lives with my family. We are among the lucky ones who go to school. We use boulders for chairs and our knees as desks. I want to get educated so that I can return home and help my people.

Life in the camp isn't easy, but there is still time to talk and laugh. One of my favorite parts of the day is when the teacher tells us one of the ancient stories about heroes, gods, and animals. She also sings songs that remind us of our home in Sudan.

Manute

Sudanese women work together to sell crops, raise children, and care for elderly relatives within the family group.

Family Life

Traditionally, the center of Sudanese life is the family. However, in the south and Darfur, many families have been torn apart by the war. Children are left without parents, while elderly relatives are left with no one to look after them.

In Sudan, parents and children are part of an extended family of grandparents, aunts, uncles, and cousins. Each family is led by a male who is responsible for all the family members. The women look after the old and the sick. They usually also take care of the home, grow crops, and collect water and firewood. The family unit works together for the protection of everyone in it, but many families have been destroyed by the war.

In Sudan, when a woman gets married, she leaves her family and becomes a part of her husband's family. In the Muslim north, families usually choose who their children will marry in arranged marriages. In the south, cattle and other gifts are given to the family of the bride as part of the wedding.

The strict Islamic laws introduced by the government in Khartoum made life particularly difficult for many women. They were told to wear the tobe, a traditional dress that covers their whole body except their face and hands. Women were also expected to stay at home. Many were fired from their jobs, and police often hassled female street traders.

This Arab Muslim girl is wearing traditional clothing that covers her face.

WOMEN AND GIRLS

During the war, women and girls suffered most from the lack of education, food, and health care. Most of the refugees in the camps were, and still are, women and children.

A WORLD APART

September 2008

Dear Manute,

    Every time I read your letter I realize how lucky I am here in peaceful Khartoum. Most days I go to an all-girls Islamic school, where the lessons are in Arabic. We study subjects such as geography and math, as well as the Quran and other holy books. I am also trying to learn some English at home. If I do well, I hope to go to college, which will help me to get a good job.

Here's the entrance to Khartoum University. Maybe I'll walk through those gates one day.

Shopping in Khartoum

Although most shops in Khartoum are small stores or market stalls, the capital's first shopping mall was built in 2007. It has a bowling alley and cinema, as well as shops and cafés.

The market is full of amazing sights and smells!

The worst part of living in Khartoum is the dust. Even in the city, sand gets everywhere. It's very hot here too, but at least I can switch on the air conditioning. In the evenings, I get to watch American shows on television. There are often power outages, but we have electricity most of the time.

We are also lucky that my father has a car, but we don't travel very far. It takes ages to wait in line for gas, and then we are hardly allowed any.

I know I shouldn't complain. Every day I think how different your life is from mine. You have spent your whole life in refugee camps and you have never even seen the village your family comes from. I hope you are able to return to your home soon.

Sittina

CHAPTER FOUR

ONE NATION BECOMES TWO

Sudan's history has shown that its wars are rarely over quickly, and peace does not always last. Although the 2005 peace deal between the southern rebels and the government held, tensions between the north and the south continued.

In January 2011, the people of the south voted to become independent from the north. As a result, Sudan was split into two countries. The north, led by President Al-Bashir, kept the name Sudan, while the south, led by President Salva Kiir, became the Republic of South Sudan.

North and South Sudan need to work together. While most of the oil fields are in the south, the oil is then piped to Port Sudan in the north.

Despite having many natural resources, the two Sudans may be among the poorest countries in the world. In addition to rich oil fields, the region has valuable minerals, such as gold, copper, and iron, which are still unexplored. The Nile is a vital source of water, and power plants along the river generate the region's electricity.

Large parts of Sudan are fertile. While most farmers raise cattle (there are 11 million cattle in the south alone), in the future they could also grow crops such as cotton, grain, and tea in suitable farming areas. Foreign companies are also beginning to invest in the area, which could also improve the prospects of the local people.

Skills such as carpentry are essential to people stricken by war. Many have had to rebuild homes and villages destroyed during the conflict.

CRAFTS AND CULTURE

Sudan has a rich and varied culture. The markets of Omdurman are home to many skilled silversmiths and leatherworkers. Nubian singers are famous for their musical skills, and the southern Sudanese are known for their wood carvings.

A New Nation

South Sudan is very remote, with few good roads. There is also a lack of food, clean water, and health care. Peace has allowed thousands of southern Sudanese to finally return home to rebuild their villages and their lives.

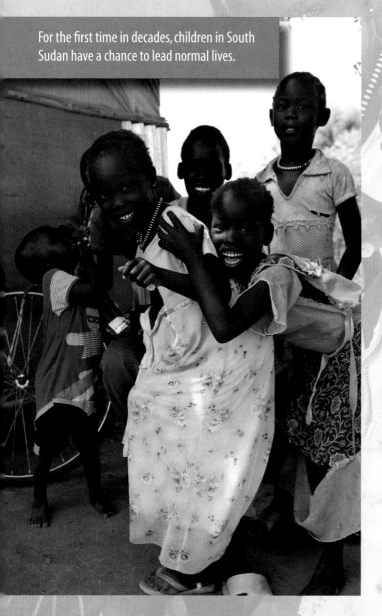

For the first time in decades, children in South Sudan have a chance to lead normal lives.

Some signs of hope are the new schools built with foreign help. More children in the south are going to school, although many find it tough to complete their studies because of a lack of funds.

Business is also starting to return to South Sudan. The country's biggest companies are mostly owned by foreigners. However, many small businesses have sprung up in the villages. These simple tin shacks include motorbike-taxi firms, milkshake stands, and stalls that charge cell phone batteries.

In addition, aid agencies are digging new wells and installing water pumps. With a good supply of water, the local farmers can cultivate their fields again.

Juba in South Sudan is the fastest-growing city in Africa. Its population has grown from 100,000 in 2005 to 1 million today. New businesses are appearing every day, from banks and cell phone companies to a brick-making factory. While life is still difficult, people are hopeful for the future.

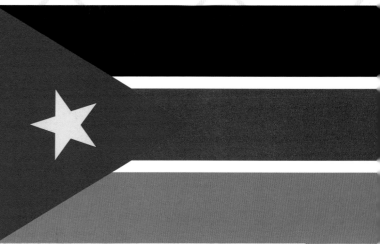

The flags of Sudan (top left) and South Sudan (top right) and a banknote from Sudan. South Sudan now has its own separate currency.

BANK OF SUDAN

Twenty Sudanese Pounds

LOST TRADITIONS

Fifty years ago, there were many more ethic groups in Sudan's countryside. However, wars and droughts have forced thousands of families to move to the cities to look for work. Many traditional ways of life have been lost forever.

HOME AT LAST!

Bahr el Ghazal, South Sudan
August 2011
Dear Sittina,

So much has happened since I last wrote to you – I don't know where to start. First of all, I should say that I am so happy! About two years ago, my family decided to return to our old village in South Sudan in a region called Bahr el Ghazal. It was incredible seeing this place for the first time, after years of hearing stories about it.

People are slowly rebuilding their homes. There are also many new projects in the area, such as digging wells, creating fish ponds, and making bricks for buildings.

A month ago, when South Sudan finally became independent from the north, there were big celebrations. At the same time, people were talking about all the relatives who died in the war. I lost an uncle, but I know it could have been a lot worse. Some people have no families at all.

I am very hopeful, but there are still many problems. Almost every day, we hear news of attacks around the country. People still struggle to feed their families. I love my country, but some days I wish I lived somewhere without fighting.

Manute

Border Dispute

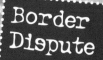

The north and south are still deciding exactly where the border between the two nations should lie. Until then, they have agreed to pull their forces away from the disputed border. However, several dangerous clashes have taken place between the two countries.

انفصال

SEPARAT

WAR

Youth for Separation
Register and vote

For Separation

There was a lot of excitement in our village leading up to the vote for separation. No one was shocked when almost everyone voted to create my new country—South Sudan.

Though the civil war is over, droughts and bad harvests still threaten many families in Sudan.

Future Challenges

Like most people, Sudanese on both sides of the border want peace, prosperity, and education. Without peace, however, the other goals are hard to achieve. Sudanese people from different cultures will first need to learn to live together.

In 2011, fighting broke out in the northern regions of Kordofan and Blue Nile, home to the Nubian people. Once more, government forces attacked unarmed villagers, mostly black Africans. Again, thousands of families were driven from their homes and land.

Meanwhile, in the south there have been several clashes between rival groups. To control the fighting, the government of South Sudan set up a new police force. In 2011, the first 5,000 recruits graduated from a new police academy. This new police presence will help to control local fighting.

Another flash point where fighting often breaks out is Abyei, which is an oil-rich region on the border between the north and south. Ethiopian troops have also helped to keep the peace there. Problems also continue in the west. Despite the 2010 cease-fire in Darfur, fighting between rebels and the janjaweed has been an ongoing problem.

A clothes stall on a rough, muddy street shows how poor much of Sudan is.

SOUTHERNERS IN THE NORTH

The vote to create South Sudan affected 700,000 southerners living in the north. They were given nine months to leave. Many families abandoned their homes and jobs to travel hundreds of miles to South Sudan. They often had to wait months to catch barges down the Nile, the only safe route south.

TWO COUNTRIES

Khartoum
October 2011
Dear Manute,
   I was so delighted to hear that you made it safely to your village. It must be incredible to be back in Sudan after so many years away.
   As you can imagine, people in Khartoum feel very differently about the split between the north and south. On the day South Sudan became independent, the streets here were very quiet. I saw some men holding Sudan's flag and cheering.

More wells bringing clean water to villages in Sudan will save a lot of lives.

The Hope for Peace

Despite all the tensions between the two sides, the presidents of both Sudan and South Sudan, Presidents Al-Bashir and Klir, have not given up. They seem determined to solve their differences and create a lasting peace. There have also been many international efforts to help, from the United Nations, South Africa, and other nations.

Our two countries can create a bright future by working together.

I am sad that the country has been split in two. We are all brothers and sisters. I hope that one day all the peoples of Sudan can learn to live together, and we can be one country again.

I'm also not sure the split will solve many problems. More and more people in our region are going hungry. Even in Khartoum, life is getting very hard. There are often protests on the streets. My father says it's because the food prices are rising too fast.

Like you, I hope things will get better. One day, when the fighting is truly over, I would love to come and visit you.

Your friend,

Sittina

GLOSSARY

African Union a group of African countries that work together to make decisions about trade and money

arranged marriage when parents decide who their child marries

civil war a war between opposing groups living in the same country

curriculum the courses studied in a particular group of schools or education system

drought a period of time during which no rain falls

ethnic group people who share the same culture

famine a severe shortage of food that can cause a large group of people to go hungry or starve

fertile rich for farming

independent when a country is not ruled by another country

invasion the takeover of a place or country, usually by military force

Islam a religion based on the teachings of the Prophet Muhammad and a belief in one god, Allah

janjaweed Arab raiders in Sudan, often armed with guns and riding on camels or horses

kidnap to take someone away and hold them against their will

mosque an Islamic place of worship and often the center of a local community, with a school or areas where people can meet up or hold feasts

natural resources raw materials that can be used to make money, such as timber (wood), fresh water, land, coal, and oil

negotiation when two or more sides try to come to an agreement

peace process efforts to bring peace to a region though negotiation rather than war

persecution the harsh and unfair treatment of a person or group

prosperity success or wealth

rebel someone who fights against something, often the government

refugees people who are forced to leave their home because of war or persecution

terrorism violent acts carried out against civilians in order to achieve a political goal

tobe traditional Sudanese dress, a wraparound cloth similar to a sari

United Nations an international organization that includes representatives of most countries in the world, and which rules in cases of international dispute

waterborne diseases diseases that are caught when people drink or wash in infected water

FOR MORE INFORMATION

Books

DiPiazza, Francesca. *Sudan in Pictures*. New York: Twenty-First Century Books, 2006.

Kavanaugh, Dorothy. *Sudan (Africa: Continent in the Balance)*. Broomall, PA: Mason Crest Publishers, 2007.

Leembruggen, Melissa. *The Sudan Project: Rebuilding with the People of Darfur*. Nashville, TN: Abingdon Press, 2007.

Williams, Mary. *Brothers in Hope: The Story of the Lost Boys of Sudan*. New York: Lee & Low Books, 2005.

Websites

www.oxfam.org.uk/coolplanet/kidsweb/world/sudan
Discover facts about Sudan and its people from one of the world's biggest charities, Oxfam.

www.enchantedlearning.com/africa/southsudan/index.shtml
Discover more about the geography, culture, and people of Sudan.

www.helpsudaninternational.org/about/index.html
Find out how organizations such as this one are helping the orphaned children of Sudan to rebuild their lives.

www.savethechildren.org
Visit the website of the charity devoted to helping children around the world. Type in the word "Sudan" to discover more about their work with children who have survived the conflict.

Publisher's note to educators and parents: Our editors have carefully reviewed these websites to ensure that they are suitable for students. Many websites change frequently, however, and we cannot guarantee that a site's future contents will continue to meet our high standards of quality and educational value. Be advised that students should be closely supervised whenever they access the Internet.

INDEX

48

4565